BLACK FRONTIERS

Even youngsters helped settle the West. These are the children of homesteaders who lived near Brownlee, Cherry County, Nebraska.

BLACK FRONTIERS

A History of African American Heroes in the Old West

by Lillian Schlissel

ALADDIN PAPERBACKS

New York   London   Toronto   Sydney   Singapore

For Rebecca and Daniel
and for Mae Fischer

First Aladdin Paperbacks edition January 2000

Text copyright © 1995 by Lillian Schlissel

Aladdin Paperbacks
An imprint of Simon & Schuster Children's Publishing Division
1230 Avenue of the Americas
New York, NY 10020

Also available in a Simon & Schuster Books for Young Readers hardcover edition.
Book design by Sylvia Frezzolini Severance.
The text for this book was set in Palatino.
Manufactured in China
30 29 28 27 26 25

The Library of Congress has cataloged the hardcover edition as follows:
Schlissel, Lillian.
Black frontiers: a history of African American heroes in the old west /
By Lillian Schlissel
p.   cm.
Includes bibliographical references and index.
Summary: Focuses on the experiences of blacks as mountain men, soldiers,
homesteaders, and scouts on the frontiers of the American West.
ISBN 0-689-80285-4 (hc.)
1. Afro-American pioneers—West (U.S.)—History-Juvenile literature. 2. Afro-American pioneers—West (U.S.)—
Biography—Juvenile literature. 3. Afro-American trappers—West (U.S.)—History—Juvenile literature.
4. Afro-American trappers—West (U.S.)—Biography-Juvenile literature. 5. Afro-American cowboys—West
(U.S.)—History—Juvenile literature. 6. Afro-American cowboys—West (U.S.)—Biography—Juvenile literature.
7. West (U.S.)—History—Juvenile literature. 8. West (U.S.)—Biography—Juvenile literature. [1. Afro-Americans—Biography
2. West (U.S.)—Biography 3. Cowboys. 4. Afro-American soldiers. 5. Frontier and pioneer life.] I. Title.
F596.3N4S35   1995   978'.00496073-dc20   92-120
ISBN 978-0-689-83315-1 (pbk.)
0622 SCP

Contents

Introduction   7

Mountain Men, Trappers, and Guides   9

Jim Beckwourth   11

Leaving the South   14

Black Homesteaders   16

The Exodusters   21

A Cowboy's Life   28

The Adventures of Nat Love   31

Bill Pickett and the Black Rodeo   36

Ned Huddleston, Alias Isom Dart,

    Alias the Black Fox   41

The Dime Novel   44

Barney Ford, Businessman   50

The Buffalo Soldiers   54

Mary Fields, "Stagecoach Mary"   60

Mary Ellen Pleasant   63

Biddy Mason   65

Black Indians   68

Conclusion   73

NOTES   74
BIBLIOGRAPHY   76
PICTURE CREDITS   78
INDEX   79

Children who lived on the prairie attended school when they weren't needed for work on the farm.

Introduction

In the days of the fur trade, black scouts and mountain men explored the continent. Later, black miners panned for gold and black families homesteaded on the Great Plains. The United States Army sent black soldiers to serve on frontier outposts. Black men and women ran businesses in frontier towns. And of the thirty-eight thousand working cowboys in the southwestern United States between 1870 and 1885, about one in four was a black man. In every way, black men and women shared the work of settling America's western frontiers.

Few black pioneers, however, left firsthand accounts of their experiences. Historians have written about black homesteaders, cowboys, and miners, and memoirs by white settlers tell of black neighbors.

The black presence in the West is sometimes most powerfully expressed in old photographs. Even when the photographs carry no names, they show how black men, women, and children forged new lives in the new country.

Black Frontiers describes experiences of some African Americans who settled the West from the end of the Civil War in 1865 to the first decades of the twentieth century.

—Lillian Schlissel

Mountain Men, Trappers, and Guides

Before 1600 North America was rich with fish, fowl, and game, and home to more than three hundred different Indian tribes. The Europeans who arrived from England, France, and the Netherlands had been sent out to bring back furs from the New World. Trappers explored waterways like the St. Lawrence and the Hudson Rivers. They organized expeditions to the Great Lakes, trading cloth, tools, liquor, and guns to the Indians for beaver and fox. Almost every expedition included black and Indian guides.

In 1803, President Thomas Jefferson sent Meriwether Lewis and William Clark to find a land route from the Missouri River to the Pacific Ocean. They traveled with a Shoshoni woman named Sacajawea, or Birdwoman, and a remarkable slave named York. Indians west of the Mississippi were fascinated by his hair and by the color of his skin, and York quickly learned several Indian languages. When the journey was over, York was given his freedom, and according to one story, he remained with the Indians, who had become his friends.

Edward Rose, part Cherokee and part black, was another famous guide and interpreter who worked for John Jacob Astor's American Fur Company. A large family named

Bonga, part black, part Chippewa, were well-known interpreters and fur traders in the Minnesota and Wisconsin Territories. It is said the family left more than one hundred descendents in that region.

Black mountain men and trappers, often part Indian, were also skilled linguists and mediators between the Indians and the Europeans, who came in increasing numbers to draw out the riches of the land.

Jim Beckwourth

Jim Beckwourth, one of the most famous of all mountain men, was born in Virginia in 1798, the son of an Irishman and a mulatto slave. Beckwourth was a jack-of-all-trades who joined his first expedition to the Rocky Mountains as a scout, hunter, and blacksmith when he was twenty-four.

Once, Beckwourth and a party of trappers were camped in the mountains when they were encircled by Blackfoot Indians. Beckwourth managed to break through the Indian lines and to come back with a rescue party. That single act made him legendary among trappers who said he had an uncanny way of following a trail.

A friend told a Crow Indian chief that Jim was the chief's long-lost son, kidnapped years before by the Cheyenne. Whether or not the story was believed, the chief invited Jim to live among the Crow Indians. Beckwourth learned the tribe's language, married a Crow woman, and became one of their leaders. After six years, he left, but he often wore Indian clothes and moccasins and kept his hair in long braids.

Beckwourth went to Florida where settlers were waging war against the Seminole tribe. This time he fought on the side of the settlers, signing on as a guide with the U.S. Army in the Seminole War.

During his lifetime, Jim Beckwourth had

Jim Beckwourth, mountain man and guide

many Indian names—Bull's Robe, Medicine Calf, Bloody Arm, Knife, and Knife-With-White-Handle. He lived with the Blackfoot, Crow, and Snake Indians, and learned what they could teach him. But at other times, he fought with the U.S. Army against Indian tribes and pledged his loyalty to white settlers.

Beckwourth worked at different jobs. On the Santa Fe Trail he ran a trading post and a saloon. In Colorado he loaded wagons. He prospected for gold and trapped big game and never stayed in one place for long.

In 1843 Beckwourth met the explorer John Charles Frémont when they were both camped in the Rocky Mountains. A few years later, Beckwourth gathered a small band of guides and trappers and joined Frémont in the Bear Flag Rebellion against Mexico for control of the California Territory. Beckwourth crossed and recrossed California's Sierra Nevada mountain range, and in 1849 when gold was discovered at Sutter's Mill, he was one of the most sought-after guides in the gold rush. Beckwourth's Pass near Reno, Nevada, was named in his honor, and Jim opened a hotel there. Guests remembered his stories of adventure, and close friends said they had seen his body covered with scars.

Jim Beckwourth died in 1866. Some believe he was poisoned by Indians who thought he had betrayed them. Others said Jim Beckwourth died peacefully at home. However he died, Beckwourth had lived a full life. He had been a trapper, scout, guide, wagon master, fighter, and interpreter. He ran a ranch, a hotel, and a saloon. He lived with some Indians and he fought against others. The frontier was full of the unexpected, and that suited Jim Beckwourth very well.

Jim Beckwourth lived with the Crow Indians and became a tribal leader.

Leaving the South

When the Civil War ended, men and women who had been slaves waited to see what freedom would bring. The land they farmed still belonged to the families who had once owned them, and because they had no money, former slaves were expected to pay back a share of their crops in exchange for seed, plows, and mules. They had to pay back a share of everything they raised for rent and food. These sharecroppers soon found they were perpetually in debt.

In 1879, a Louisiana sharecropper named John Lewis Solomon, his wife, and four children packed their belongings and started walking toward the Mississippi River. Along the riverbank they found other black families waiting for a chance to travel north. Some built rafts to carry them over the river's dangerous undertows and eddies. Others had money for passage, but riverboat captains would not let them on board. When a steamboat called the *Grand Tower* came close to shore, John Lewis Solomon called to the captain that he could pay his way. He said he had been a soldier in the Union Army. "I know my rights, and if you refuse to carry me on your boat, I will go to the United States Court and sue for damages." Solomon took a great risk, but the captain agreed to let him and his family board the steamboat.

Black families waited on the banks of the Mississippi River for a chance to go north.

Reaching Kansas, Solomon said, "This is free ground. Then I looked on the heavens, and I said, 'That is free and beautiful heaven.' Then I looked within my heart, and I said to myself, 'I wonder why I was never free before'."[1]

Black Homesteaders

Homesteading was not easy for black or white settlers. Rocks, grass, and trees had to be cleared before crops could be planted. A farmer needed a horse, a mule, and a plow. He needed seed to plant and food for his family until the crops were ready to harvest. Most of all a pioneer needed a home.

In regions where there were trees, pioneers built log cabins. But in Kansas and Nebraska, there was only tall grass, as high as a man's shoulder. Pioneers learned that tough root systems under the grass held the dirt firmly, and sod could be cut like bricks and piled, layer upon layer, until it took the shape of a house. These homesteaders were called sod busters, and their homes were called soddies.

Sod homes could be warm and comfortable. Some were two stories high, with glass windows and chimneys. But in heavy rain, smaller sod houses leaked, and some families remembered being surprised by a snake slithering through a wall.

In North and South Dakota, where the land was rocky and winter temperatures fell to 30 degrees below zero, early pioneers burrowed into the ground and covered themselves with an earthen roof. They brought their small ani-

Loading sod for a house on the Dismal River, Thomas County, Kansas

mals into the house in the winter, while cows and goats huddled on the roof, warming themselves on the house that was under their feet.

During the first seasons in a new settlement, a pioneer woman might have no stove.

She dug a hole in the ground and fed the fire with weeds, adding small rocks, like coals, to keep in the fire's heat. Buffalo chips, the droppings of buffalo, provided the fuel. When the great animals migrated across the land, women

Dugout on the South Loup River, near Virge Allen's homestead, Custer County, Nebraska, 1892.
A wagon load of sod stands by to repair the roof.

and children gathered chips for the family's cooking fires.

In the hot and dry climate of the Southwest, pioneers built homes with thick walls made of mud and straw. The mud walls, called adobe, kept the houses cool in the summer and warm in the winter. In desert regions, women learned from the Indians to brew teas out of wild grasses and to make soap and shampoo from the yucca plant.

Ada McColl, 1893, gathering buffalo chips near Lakin, Kansas

In the early days of settlement, there were few black families homesteading. For them, loneliness was part of being a pioneer. But black pioneer families held on, and in sticking it out, they made the way easier for those who came after.

ABOVE: *For black pioneer families, homesteading was a desolate life.*

LEFT: *Unidentified child on the Maurice Brown homestead in Nebraska*

The Exodusters

Men and women who had been slaves read in the Bible about the ancient Israelites who were brought out of bondage and delivered into freedom. Benjamin Singleton, born a slave in Tennessee, was determined that he would bring his people to free soil if it was the last thing he ever did.

After the Civil War, Singleton visited Kansas and over a period of years, he and his friends managed to buy part of a Cherokee reservation. In 1877 they advertised for homesteaders to start an all-black community there. They hoped to attract two hundred families. Fliers promised that settlers who paid one dollar "in installments of 25 cents at a time or otherwise as may be desired" could be part of the new community. By 1879 an exodus of black families out of the Old South began, and before long there were eight hundred homesteaders in the new Kansas communities of Dunlap and Nicodemus. Benjamin Singleton said, "My people that I carried to Kansas came on our own resources. We have tried to make a people of ourselves. . . ."[2] They were known as the Exodusters.

Farmers in Nicodemus owned only three horses. One man plowed with a milk cow, and others broke ground with shovels and spades. White farmers saw how hard their new neigh-

LEFT: *Benjamin Singleton, founder of the black community of Dunlap, Kansas*

ABOVE: *Handbills encouraged black families to move to Kansas. Notice the warning at the bottom of the flier.*

bors worked and lent the new settlers a team of oxen and a plow. Black farmers planted their first crops and in time they prospered. By the turn of the century there were about eight thousand black homesteaders in Nicodemus and Dunlap.

Some black settlers moved farther west to Nebraska and Oklahoma where they built three new black communities—Taft, Langston, and Boley. George Washington Bush went all the way to Oregon Territory where he introduced the first mower and reaper into the area around Puget Sound.

Of all the black communities, however,

Schoolhouse in Dunlap, Kansas. Pupil in foreground carries a sign that reads, "God Bless Our School."

The Shores family in front of their sod house near Westville, Custer County, Nebraska, 1887.
The Shores became famous as musicians.

The Moses Speese family—neighbors of the Shores family—outside their sod house near Westville, Custer County, Nebraska

Nicodemus and Dunlap remained the most famous. Each year they celebrated the Fourth of July, and they had their own special holiday, Emancipation Day. On July 31 and August 1, a square mile of land was set aside as a carnival fairground. There were boxing matches and baseball games. In 1907 the town formed one of the nation's first black baseball teams—the Nicodemus Blues. The Blues played black teams as far away as Texas, Nevada, and Louisiana. Satchell Paige, one of the greatest black pitchers in American baseball history, played ball in Nicodemus.

In 1976 Nicodemus was designated a National Historic Landmark. The town's history is being recorded and buildings restored. It marks the proud legacy of black homesteaders in America.[3]

This black baseball team played for the Pullman Club Saloon in Tonepah, Nevada, 1907.

Bill Houston • Bert Wakefield • Twity McAdoo • West Wilkins • Bill Lindsey • Tom McCampbell • Chick Pollam • Frank Evans • Tom Starman • Ernest McCampbell • Fred Lee • Ray Lindsey

Kansas City Monarchs, 1908

Satchell Paige, one of baseball's greatest pitchers, playing for the Kansas City Monarchs, 1908

A Cowboy's Life

Most boys dream of becoming cowboys. They see themselves on a fine horse, wearing a gun belt and spurs. But to westerners in the 1880s, a cowboy was just "a bowlegged man who sleeps in his underwear."

A cowboy might spend two or three months in the saddle, moving twenty-five hundred head of longhorn cattle over a thousand miles of rough land covered with mesquite and roving coyotes. A long cattle drive would start in Texas and end in one of the Kansas "cow towns" of Abilene, Wichita, or Dodge City. Here the cattle were loaded onto boxcars and carried by railroad to Chicago for slaughter.

Crossing open land almost always meant emergencies. A river at flood time could overturn wagons. A drowning, panic-stricken calf might kill the cowboy trying to save it. Flat stretches of land concealed rocks and holes that could trip even a sure-footed horse. The bite of a rattlesnake could penetrate a cowboy's boot. Then his only chance would be to cut the flesh between the fang marks and suck out the venom. Some cowboys poured gunpowder on the wound to counteract the poison.

On a perfectly calm day, a herd might stampede. In a land without fences, cattle got mixed up. Rustlers were always changing or tampering with brands and gunplay was common.

Lightning could frighten cattle, and some cowboys swore that they saw balls of fire on the ends of longhorns in a storm.

> The water poured down in sheets and barrels. It rained blue snakes, pitchforks and bob-tailed heifer yearlings all at once. One minute was darker than the dead end of a crooked tunnel a mile deep under a mountain. Then the prairie was a sea of blue and yellow light dazzling to all eyes.[4]

Prairie fires spread havoc over dry land. One tactic was to start a second fire to counter the first. When that didn't work, desperate cowboys might slaughter their cattle, split open the bloody carcasses, and drag them along the fire line in a last-ditch effort to dampen the ground.

Dust storms on the trail covered cowboys with dust an inch thick and left them half blind. When water barrels filled up with dust, cowboys said they had to chew the "black stuff" before they could swallow it.

On icy nights, winds stung hands and faces, and if the herd was hit with a snow-

The Stampede, *a painting by Frederic Remington*

storm, horses and cattle had to be brought to a shelter before they froze.

As dangerous as a cowboy's life could be, scores of young black men left the South when the Civil War ended. They headed west on dirt roads, from Alabama and South Carolina to Texas. Even as slaves, blacks had worked cattle on horseback in Southern states. When they reached Texas, they found ranchers who were glad to hire them.

Between 1870 and 1885 there were about thirty-eight thousand working cowboys in the United States. Historians estimate that one in four was a black man. They were paid the same wages as white and Mexican workers and enjoyed a degree of camaraderie and freedom. At a time when black sharecroppers were being lynched by the Ku Klux Klan in the South, black cowboys in Texas and Colorado enjoyed a rough equality in ranch life.[5]

A cowboy was expected to find every calf, no matter what the weather.

The Adventures of Nat Love

Nat Love was one of the few black cowboys to write the story of his own life. His autobiography was entitled *The Life and Adventures of Nat Love*. Born on a slave plantation in Tennessee in 1854, he ran off to Dodge City, Kansas, when he was fifteen. As a herd of cattle thundered through the main street of the town, Nat spied a black cowboy and asked for a job. Bronco Jim hired Nat and bought him a saddle, bridle, spurs, blankets, and a Colt .45 revolver. Nat was to earn thirty dollars a month in cowboy pay.

In Texas he was trained to be a brand reader. His job was to brand the calves, to keep his herd from mixing with other herds on the trail, and to make certain the brands were not tampered with by rustlers.

Sometimes cowboy life was exciting, but weeks on the trail could also be dull. Nat told how cowboys kept themselves entertained when they didn't have much to do:

> A big long-horn wild steer, generally the worst in the herd, was cut out and turned loose on the open prairie. . . . As the steer was separated from its fellows [he] would become extremely ferocious and wild, and the man who attempted to rope and ride him would be in momentary danger of losing his life.

Nat Love, sometimes known as Deadwood Dick

I have seen two horses and their riders gored to death in the sport, and I have had to shoot more than one steer to save myself and my horse.[6]

Nat Love was an expert roper and rider, and on July 4, 1876, in Deadwood, South Dakota, he won every single event in a rodeo contest. The people were so impressed they gave him the name of the town as a prize. From then on, he had the right to be called Deadwood Dick. Nat wrote, "I have always carried the name with honor."[7]

Once, when Nat Love was searching the prairie for lost cattle, he was captured by Indians. It was October 1876, only a few months after the Sioux defeated General George Armstrong Custer at the Battle of the Little Bighorn in Montana. Nat did not tell which tribe took him prisoner, but he noticed that the Indians had "a large percentage of colored blood in the tribe."[8] At that moment, being a black man probably saved his life.

The Indians adopted him and gave him the name Buffalo Papoose. Then they pierced his ears.

They had a small bone secured from a deer's leg, a small thin bone, rounded at the end and as sharp as a needle. This they used to make the holes, then strings made from the tendons of a deer were inserted in place of thread . . . earrings were placed in my ears and salve made from herbs [was] placed on my wounds.[9]

Nat Love lived with the Indians and learned some astonishing things about their skills.

Their shields were made of tanned buffalo skins and so tough that an arrow would not pierce them . . . Neither will a bullet pierce them unless the ball hits the shield square on, otherwise it glances off.[10]

Eventually, Nat longed to return to his life as a cowboy. One night he crawled to the corral, picked a fast pony, sprang on its back, and rode for his life. Perhaps the Indians could not catch him, or perhaps they let him ride away.

Back in Texas, Nat Love had a different kind of adventure. The cowboys were bringing in stray calves when Nat's horse suddenly threw him to the ground and galloped away. He held on to his Winchester rifle and his saddle, but the saddle weighed forty pounds and Nat could hardly carry it. He staggered on until he came across a herd of buffalo, and there among the buffalo was one of the lost calves. But it was no time for sentimentality. Nat wrote that he killed the calf and drank its blood.[11]

He was so exhausted, he hardly noticed that the temperature had dropped below freezing. Snow soon blanketed the country. When Nat awoke, one hand was frozen around the Winchester and the other around the horn of his saddle. His friends found him just in time, but despite all they could do, the skin came off his nose and mouth, and his hands and feet were so badly frozen, the nails came off. Nat once said, "I will never forget those few days when I was lost, and the marks of that storm I will carry with me always."[12]

In the spring of 1877, Nat Love and his friends were back in Dodge City, Kansas. They were drinking in a saloon and rode out of town feeling reckless. As Nat galloped along, he saw an old cannon just inside the gates of Fort Dodge, and he decided to take it back with him to Texas. Making for the cannon at full speed, Nat threw his lariat out and watched it encircle the cannon. "Then putting spurs to my horse, I tried to drag the cannon after me." [13]

The soldiers inside the fort sounded the alarm and ran for their horses and rifles. Nat tried to make a run for it, but of course the cannon wouldn't move, and he was captured and thrown into the guard house.

The famous gunfighter Bat Masterson heard that Nat Love tried to lasso a cannon, and he convinced the soldiers to let Nat go free. But from then on, cowboys reminded Nat of the time he tried to drag a cannon all the way from Kansas to Texas at the end of a rope.

By 1890 the frontier was disappearing, and the days of the long cattle drives were over.

Railroad tracks extended into Texas, and cattle could be loaded directly onto railroad cars. Longhorn cattle were a vanishing breed. The huge span of their horns—five to eight feet from one horn tip to the other—made them too difficult to load onto boxcars. Ranchers began raising smaller-horned breeds like Hereford and Angus, which produced beef more to America's taste. The law caught up with gunfighters like William Bonney, known as Billy the Kid. Most were shot or hanged. And the forty million buffalo that roamed the land were slaughtered by homesteaders and ranchers. By the end of the century, there were fewer than one thousand buffalo left in the whole country. In 1913, when the U.S. Mint coined the first buffalo nickel, with the head of a bison on one side and an Indian chief on the other, the design was made by an artist from a buffalo in New York's Central Park Zoo. The Indian head was a composite drawn from portraits of three different tribal leaders.

The West was filling up with towns and

cities, and Nat Love changed with the times. He took a job with the railroad, and though he loved the big locomotives, he noted in his autobiography that he always remembered

the countless thousands of long horn steers, the wild mustangs. The buffalo and other game, the Indians, the delight of living outdoors and the fights against death that caused every nerve to tingle, and the everyday communion with men whose minds were as broad as the plains they roamed and whose creed was every man for himself and every friend for each other and with each other till the end.[14]

In 1890 Nat Love left the cowboy life behind to become a Pullman porter on the Denver and Rio Grande Railroad.

Bill Pickett and the Black Rodeo

Bill Pickett was one of the most famous rodeo riders of all times. Tradition has it that his family was part black, part white, and part Cherokee. Bill's father, Thomas Jefferson Pickett, worked on ranches north of Austin, Texas, and Bill spent his youth watching cowboys work. One day, he saw a "cow dog" pull out a frightened cow hiding in a thicket. The dog went up to the cow and bit its lip. The cow was so startled it stood perfectly still, and the dog led it gently within reach of the cowboys.

If a dog could stop a grown cow, perhaps a man could do the same. Bill tried the trick on a calf. He grabbed the calf's ears and twisted its head. Then, just as he had seen the dog do, he bit the calf's lip. The calf held still, and Bill flipped it over and threw it to the ground.

Bill practiced the trick again and again. Soon he learned to ride a galloping horse, spring from its back, wrestle a steer to the ground, and bite its lip until it rested in stunned surprise.

Pickett began performing the trick at county fairs. In the 1890s, Bill and his brothers formed the Pickett Brothers Bronco Busters and Rough Riders Association. By 1903, he was bulldogging in rodeos throughout Texas and Arizona. A newspaper reporter who watched him ride in Cheyenne, Wyoming, wrote:

. . . Pickett . . . mounted on a horse and caught up with the steer that had been turned loose a little in advance of his start. There were many in the audience who thought that it would be impossible for a man to throw a steer with his teeth and the interest became intense. The silence of expectation which settled on the grandstand as the horse drew near the lumbering brute deepened to a dead calm as the Negro's horse dashed alongside the animal, catching the stride of the steer, and then the Negro leaped from the horse to the steer's back. Pickett wound himself around the animal's neck and fastened his teeth in its upper lip.

Then, with a series of quick jerking movements, [Pickett] forced the steer to its knees, then it rolled over on its side. The immense crowd cheered . . . and he again jumped on the back of the steer, which regained its feet, and repeated the performance.[15]

In 1905 Bill Pickett joined the 101 Wild West Show. The 101 Ranch spread out across 101,000 acres of Oklahoma Territory. But some said it

Bill Pickett and his horse Spradley

got its name because it was 101 miles from Oklahoma City, 101 miles from Tulsa, and 101 miles from Wichita. Ranch owners were determined to put Oklahoma on the map, and they decided to stage a huge rodeo for the general public and for newspaper reporters and editors. Thirty trains brought sixty-five thousand people to the 101 Ranch for a roundup. There was a grand parade led by the Oklahoma Territory Cavalry Band. Geronimo, the old Apache chief, led two hundred Indians in war paint from seven different tribes. Geronimo was officially a prisoner of the Army, but he had been promised he could kill one last buffalo before he died. Among the cowboys was Tom Mix, who would later star in Hollywood movies, and Lucille Mulhall, America's First Cowgirl, who performed on her trained horse, Governor. Dozens of ranch hands pretended to be homesteaders in ox-drawn wagons, and the audience watched as the frontier became an afternoon's entertainment.

Geronimo killed his last buffalo, which was cooked and served to the editors, and there were bronco riders and roping contests. Then Bill Pickett, billed as the "Dusky Demon," rode his horse Spradley, into the ring. He leaped onto a thousand-pound steer, "grasped a horn in each of his hands, dug his heels into the ground . . . and began to twist its neck. . . . He sank his teeth into the steer's tender upper lip," and bit down hard. The steer fell on its side, and the crowd rose with a roar of approval.[16]

Bill Pickett and the 101 Wild West Show toured the United States, Canada, South America, and Great Britain. In 1907, the 101 included ninety cowboys and cowgirls, seventy Indians, and three hundred horses, buffalo, and longhorn cattle. They performed before thousands of people.

In 1923 Pickett played himself in a silent movie called *The Bull-Dogger*, but there were not enough black movie-goers in the days of silent films for Bill to become a successful Hollywood cowboy like Tom Mix, who made 370 western movies and more than six million dollars.

In 1932 Bill Pickett died when he was kicked by a wild horse.

Almost forty years later, in 1971, Bill Pickett was inducted into the National Rodeo Cowboy Hall of Fame by western movie star Joel McCrea. He was the twentieth man selected, and the first and only black cowboy to be awarded a place in the Western Heritage Center in Oklahoma City. In 1987 a bronze statue of Pickett bulldogging a steer was unveiled at the Fort Worth Cowtown Coliseum.[17]

Jesse Stahl, riding his horse Glasseye, was another spectacular black performer with grace and split-second timing.

The Negro Rodeo Association was formed by black cowboys in Houston, Texas, in 1947, and since then there have been six different associations of black rodeo performers. Today the Bill Pickett Invitational Rodeo is held annually in Denver, Colorado, and the Black World Championship Rodeo is held at the 369th Armory at 143rd Street and Lenox Avenue in

Jesse Stahl riding his horse Glasseye, 1916

Arthur L. Walker, cowboy

New York City. Coast to coast, there are more than five hundred rodeos each year. Rodeo, along with basketball, baseball, and automobile racing, has become one of the nation's leading spectator sports. Black riders like Bill Pickett and Jesse Stahl set a standard of performance that is remembered by rodeo riders across the country.

Second rodeo of Colored Rodeo Association, Denver, Colorado, 1948

Ned Huddleston, Alias Isom Dart, Alias the Black Fox

One of the very best bronco riders of all time was Ned Huddleston. "No man in the country understood horses better than [he] did." No better rider "ever threw a leg over a horse."[18]

Huddleston was born a slave in Arkansas in 1849. At sixteen he ran away and joined a rodeo in Mexico, where he learned to be a stunt rider and a clown. A rodeo clown is hired to make audiences laugh, but his most important job is to protect a cowboy who has fallen off his horse. It takes daring and skill to draw off an angry bull from a cowboy who is hurt on the ground.

Ned was a natural. He could saddle a horse when no other man could come near it. Rodeo riders said they had seen Ned talk to horses. On occasion it was also said he talked a horse away from its owner.

When Huddleston came back to the United States, he tried mining, but white men were almost always stealing whatever gold a black man found. So Ned went back to working with horses, or rather, to stealing horses. He joined some thieves known throughout the Southwest as the Gault Gang. They would stampede a herd of horses and ride off with as many as they could get to follow them.

*Isom Dart, bronco rider and
sometime rustler*

The owner of one herd laid an ambush at the rustlers' camp, and when the thieves returned, he and his men killed every single one.

When Ned came back to the hideout, he saw the bodies of his friends. It was a sobering sight. After emptying their money belts, he gave each man a decent burial. When night fell, Ned worried that the men who killed the gang might come back for him, and so he slipped into one of the new graves and spent the night next to a dead man.

In the light of morning, Ned got on a train headed for Oklahoma. When he got off the train, he changed his name to Isom (sometimes Isham) Dart and decided it was time to go straight.

Yet, whether his name was Ned Huddleston or Isom Dart, Ned didn't exactly change his ways. He found a new gang and went on living by a little "larceny of livestock." In other words, he stole a few more horses.

It wasn't long before Isom Dart was arrested. On the way to jail, the sheriff's horse bolted, the buckboard turned over, and the sheriff's leg was broken. Now Isom may have been a horse thief, but he was also a kindhearted man. He caught the horses, righted the buckboard, took the sheriff to a doctor, and turned himself in at the local jail.

When Isom Dart came to trial, the all-white jury said he was an honest man, and they set him free.

Dart went to work breaking wild horses. That meant getting them to tolerate a bridle and saddle. People who watched him work began to call him "the Black Fox."

After years of hard work, Ned Huddleston finally saved enough money to buy his own ranch. But just as Ned—or Isom—was settling down, a paid killer named Tom Horn began hunting men who had once been horse rustlers.

Ned was going straight and paid little attention to warnings, but one day, as he stepped out of the door of his own cabin, he was gunned down.

How should Ned Huddleston be remembered? As one of the best bronco riders in the West? Or as a horse thief and rustler? Perhaps he should be thought of as a superb horseman, a black cowboy with a good heart, a man who loved wild horses and life just a little outside the law.

The Dime Novel

As the old frontier disappeared and cowboys took jobs with the railroads, western adventure found new life in magazines and in dime novels. A dime novel was something like today's comic books, and if you couldn't afford a dime, you could buy a story from the Half Dime Library for five cents. These little magazines, which were generally about fifteen pages long, were published in New York City just before the Civil War by Erastus Beadle. Nearly five million copies were sold between 1860 and 1865. Some of the heroes of the dime novels are still remembered today—Deadwood Dick, Hurricane Nell, Calamity Jane, and Buffalo Bill.

Prentiss Ingraham wrote more than six hundred adventures for the series. Most of the stories followed a formula in which a young boy went west to find fortune and adventure. He was called the Boy Detective, or the Boy Buccaneer, or the Boy Bugler, or the Boy Smuggler. The boy hero was brave and daring, and he always took care of his mother.

In the story of *Arizona Joe*, the hero is Joe Bruce. He and his mother live in New York City until one day when Joe announces he is going to Texas to become a cowboy. Though he is a city boy, he is an able horseman and an expert shot with pistols and rifles. In Texas, Joe becomes a scout, an Indian fighter, and a miner. What is of special interest, however, is his meeting with "Texas Jack" Omohundro, who wore deerskin trousers and carried two butcher knives and a rifle. Jack's partner was a black man known as the Ebony Star.

Once, when Joe Bruce is pursued by a dozen Indians, his horse stumbles and throws its rider to the ground. Texas Jack and Star watch from the top of the ridge as the Indians come closer, and then they stage a dramatic rescue. The dime novel tells the story this way:

❧ ARIZONA JOE ❧
The Boy Pard of Texas Jack

CHAPTER X
TEXAS JACK

A few moments before this fall of Joe's pony, two horsemen rode up to the top of the ridge which the boy was striving so hard to reach.

One was a white man, the other a negro.

The former was a man of thirty, with a handsome, fearless face, bronzed almost to the hue of a red-skin, and with eyes very bright and restless.

His chestnut hair was wavy and worn long, falling upon his broad shoulders. His form was athletic, indicating great strength and endurance.

He was clad in buckskin leggings and hunting shirt; he wore cavalry boots, armed with Mexican spurs, and upon his head was a broad-brimmed sombrero, ornamented with a diamond five-point star in the front, and on the left side of the hat crown was an eagle embroidered in gold, while an ingeniously made rattlesnake-skin, looking life like, made the hat-band.

His horse was a splendid black animal, the trappings being Mexican. His arms were a silver-mounted, repeating rifle, revolvers and knife, a gold star being set in each weapon.

His black companion was a giant in size, with a face that was full of character.

He also was dressed in buckskin, wearing moccasins instead of boots, and carried a repeating rifle, revolvers and knife. His sombrero was looped up with a gold star, and his horse was a large roan, his trappings being Mexican.

"Ah! There's a race for life, Star," cried the white man, as he reached the top of the ridge and beheld Joe flying at full speed and the Indians in pursuit.

"Yes, Massa Jack, and he looks like a young feller, too," responded the negro.

"True; he appears to be but a boy, so we'll chip in, Star, or those red devils will catch him, sure as my name is Texas Jack."

"They will, for sart'in, sah."

Down the ridge the two rode and had reached the thicket at the bottom just as Joe's horse went down.

"He's down, Massa Jack!"

"So I see. Push on, Star, and rattle your rifle as you ride. I will pass the boy, but you pick him up and bring him back to the ridge here, and I will follow to cover the retreat. Now for it."

With a yell that was well-known to the red riders, Texas Jack dashed out of the thicket, and close by his side was Star, the ebony giant.

The red-skins were nonplused at first, and momentarily drew rein, but seeing only two enemies they dashed on again, determined to reach the boy and get his arms and scalp.

The silent form lying upon the prairie might be dead, but the red-skins should not have his scalp, so the daring scout decided.

Star, as ordered, opened fire with his rifle as they charged, and being a repeater, it rattled out the shots in a lively way.

An Indian fell from his horse, and a horse went down under the fusillade.

Then Jack opened fire, shooting slowly but surely, and when he had dropped four red-skins from their saddles, the balance turned and they hurried off out of range of that dreadful "long-talk gun."

One of those killed was the chief. His horse dashed near Jack, who, as he passed, seized the ever-ready lariat from the horn of his saddle and caught the animal, which proved to be a truly splendid mustang.

But what of the Ebony Star?

A prodigious feat he performed while Texas Jack rode beyond and held the savages at bay with his terrible rifle.

Still seated in his saddle, his repeating rifle hung at his back, the giant leaned forward and over, as the big horse dashed up to the unconscious boy and, as he passed, the limp body was seized, and Star sat erect, in an instant, with Joe clasped in his right hand.

Then he turned the horse's head back toward

the cover of the wood, while Jack rode back to the spot where the poor, wounded pony now lay, and, seeing its leg was broken, mercifully put a bullet in its brain, and slowly retreated to the thicket, where Star had preceded him.

Once in the thicket he dismounted, and approached Star, who was now bending over the boy, looking anxiously in Joe's pale and pain-marked face.

"He's not dead, Star?" asked Jack.

"No, sah; he have bled free from this arrow wound, and he struck his head on the prairie, fer you see it's scratched here, sah, and it stunned him, but I guess he'll be all right soon, for the arrow wasn't p'izened."

"That is good. He's a handsome fellow, Star, and cannot be over sixteen. Look after him, Star. You are a good doctor, as I well know. I'll have to start those red-skins off again, as they look as though they meant to give us trouble for the loss of their chief, whom I brought down the first shot."

"Yas, sah. I'll look arter him, sah," responded the giant, and Texas Jack rode out upon the prairie toward the red-skins, who had halted in a group some distance off.

As he approached they fell back, for they well knew the long range of his deadly rifle, and putting spurs to his horse, he caught the Indian pony that was running loose.

The red-skins gave a yell at this, but, unheeding it, Texas Jack stripped the dead Indians and ponies of their arms and trappings, and rode quietly back toward the ridge.

CHAPTER XI

THE SCOUT'S PROTEGE

"How is the lad, Star?" quietly asked Texas Jack, as he entered the thicket.

"He's come to, sah, but I guess he's kinder out o' his head a leetle."

* * *

"Now, Star, we must leave the ridge at once," said Jack.

Lifting Joe in his strong arms, he handed him to the negro, and leading the captured ponies, they set off on their way to their lonely ranch, twenty miles distant.

* * *

It was midnight when at last Texas Jack and Star, bearing his burden, rode up to a clump of timber several acres in size. In it was a stockade fence forming an enclosure of half an acre, and in one end of this was a cabin stoutly built of logs.

This was the prairie home of Texas Jack, many a long mile away from the nearest settlement, and here he dwelt alone with Star.

* * *

Texas Jack had a small case of medicines, and the two did all in their power for the poor boy, nursing him day after day until at last the fever was broken and reason returned.

"I am not dead, then," said Joe one day, looking curiously about him.

Texas Jack was away on a scout, and Star was seated just outside of the cabin napping.

He started as he heard the voice of his patient, and entering the cabin said:

"No, sah. You has been very sick, though."

"Where am I?"

"In Texas."

"I think I remember. I was running from some Indians, and my horse fell with me."

"Yes, sah, and broke his leg."

"Poor fellow; but I thought, when I hit the ground that he had broken my neck."

"No, sah, but he stunned yer considerable."

"Is my scalp safe?" and Joe raised his hand weakly to his head.

"Oh, yas, sah, it's all safe and you is getting along prime and must be cheerful and build up."

* * *

"Did I kill any Indians?" asked Joe with a slight shudder.

"Massa Jack said you did, sah, for he followed yer trail back to the timber on the stream, and found whar you had kilt an Injun, and his pony."

"Who is Jack?" wearily asked Joe.

"Massa Texas Jack, sah."

"Texas Jack!" and Joe brightened up.

"Yes, sah, this is his cabin, and we seen you when you fell, and Massa Jack and me beat the Injuns off and fetched up here, and you has been three weeks sick almost."

When Joe awoke, the famous scout stood by his side and said in his frank way: "My lad, you must get well now, for I'm going to make you my PROTEGE, for I met Pathfinder the guide this morning, and he told me all about you. Get well now for you are to be the Boy Pard of Texas Jack."

Not many other books before 1900 showed friendships between a white man and a black man. In real life, black cowboys did not call their partners Massa, and Texas Jack did not call Joe Bruce his Boy Pard or his protege. Literary conventions get in the way. The story of *Arizona Joe* is unusual because in it a black man, Star, rescues the hero, Joe Bruce, and saves his life. As with the Lone Ranger and Tonto, the Ebony Star is Texas Jack's powerful friend and ally. Along with Ned Huddleston, the Black Fox, and Bill Pickett, the Dusky Demon, Star has a place in the legends of the Old West.

Front cover of dime novel Arizona Joe

Barney Ford, Businessman

Barney Ford escaped his slave owners and made his way to Chicago even before the Civil War ended. There he met Henry Wagoner, who worked for a newspaper founded by the black leader Frederick Douglass. Wagoner was a member of the Underground Railroad, a secret organization formed to help slaves escape. In time, Barney Ford married Wagoner's sister, Julia, and when gold was discovered in California in 1849, the newlyweds decided to find their fortunes out west.

To reach California, Barney and his wife took a train to New York, and then a ship down the Atlantic Coast to Central America.

Before the Panama Canal was opened in 1914, travelers disembarked in Nicaragua and took a carriage or a mule train across the narrow strip of land until they reached the Pacific Coast. Then they boarded another ship and sailed north to San Francisco. Barney Ford studied the weary travelers and decided to open a hotel in Nicaragua so people could rest and enjoy some American food before continuing their journey. Ford never reached California, but he went back to Chicago a rich man.

When gold was discovered in Colorado ten years later, Barney Ford decided to try his luck again. He was rich enough this time to afford a seat on a stagecoach, but blacks were not permitted to ride. Barney was never a man to be deterred. He found a wagon train and signed on as a barber.

When he reached Mountain City, Colorado, Ford, who had once owned a hotel, found no one would rent him a room. Clara Brown, a black woman who had come to Colorado as a laundress, saw to it that he had a place to stay, and then she introduced him to black business-men, who owned a smelting company, a bakery, and a newspaper. Soon, Barney and five of his new friends staked a claim and started prospecting for gold. They could hardly believe their luck when they found what they were looking for.

Ford and his friends asked a white lawyer to file their claim, but a sheriff in league with the lawyer ordered the black miners off their own land and stole their gold.

Perhaps, though, the black miners had the last laugh. The sheriff and the lawyer kept looking for more gold, under the floor boards,

Black and white miners prospecting in Spanish Flat, California, 1852

Black prospector, Auburn Ravine, California, 1852

near the well, even around the outhouse. No one except Barney Ford and his friends ever found gold on that claim.

When Barney left the mining camps, he managed to keep enough gold dust to go back to Denver and, with his old friend Henry Wagoner, to open a string of businesses—barber shops, restaurants, and hotels. Barney built and managed the huge Inter Ocean Hotel in Cheyenne, Wyoming, and later Ford's Hotel in Denver. Though each hotel burned down, Ford rebuilt them and started again.

Barney Ford and Henry Wagoner worked within the black community of Denver, setting up the first adult classes to teach reading, writing, arithmetic, and government. Ford was the first black man to serve on a grand jury in Colorado, and Wagoner was the first to be a deputy sheriff. In 1964 Denver changed the name Nigger Hill, where Ford discovered gold, to Barney Ford Hill.[19] It was a way for the city to honor a respected citizen.

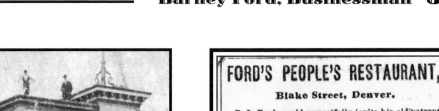

FORD'S PEOPLE'S RESTAURANT,

Blake Street, Denver.

B. L. Ford would respectfully invite his old patrons and the public generally to call and see him at his new and commodious

Saloon, Restaurant and Barber Shop,

on the site of his old stand. Gentlemen will find at ALL HOURS his tables supplied with the

MOST CHOICE AND DELICATE LUXURIES OF COLORADO AND THE EAST.

Private parties of Ladies and Gents can be accommodated with special meals, and Oyster Suppers to order, in his upstairs saloon.

HIS BAR IS STOCKED WITH

The Very Finest Liquors and Cigars

that gold or greenbacks can control of first hands in the eastern markets. Denver and Mountain Lager received daily.

Game of all kinds, Trout, &c., constantly on hand for regular and transient customers, and served up in a style second to no other restaurant in the west.

A Shaving and Hairdressing Saloon

is connected with the establishment, in the basement, wherein competent artists are ever pleased to wait on customers in first class style.

Our motto is to please and satisfy.   aug26dtf

LEFT: *Ford's Hotel on Fifteenth Street, Denver, Colorado* ABOVE: *Advertisement for Ford's Restaurant, Saloon, and Barber Shop in Denver, Colorado*

The Buffalo Soldiers

During the Civil War, nearly 180,000 black troops fought with the Union Army against the Confederacy, and more than 33,000 gave their lives to end slavery. After the war, General Ulysses S. Grant ordered Generals Philip Sheridan and William Tecumseh Sherman to organize regiments of black cavalry. These were designated the Ninth and Tenth Cavalry, each containing about a thousand men under the command of white commissioned officers—Colonel Edward Hatch for the Ninth and Colonel Benjamin Grierson for the Tenth. Two black regiments of infantry were organized, the Twenty-fourth and the Twenty-fifth. George Armstrong Custer refused to command black troops, but others accepted their tasks gladly.

Black troops who had been farmers, cooks, carpenters, and blacksmiths came from all parts of the country. The Army paid them thirteen dollars a month plus rations and sent them to the most desolate and dangerous frontier outposts where they served under the harshest conditions with the oldest equipment. They fought Indian tribes few soldiers wished to encounter—the Cheyenne, Comanche, Kiowa, Apache, Ute, and Sioux.

It was the Indians who gave the black troops the name Buffalo Soldiers because their hair resembled the shaggy coats of the buffalo.

Regimental insignia, Tenth Calvary, Buffalo Soldiers

The buffalo was sacred to the Indians, and the men of the Ninth and Tenth Cavalry and the Twenty-fourth and Twenty-fifth Infantry accepted the name as a badge of honor, and the buffalo became a prominent part of their regimental crest.

Thirteen men of the Buffalo Soldiers won the highest military award of the nation, the Congressional Medal of Honor.

When all-black regiments were disbanded after World War II, almost one hundred years after they were organized, the Tenth Cavalry became the 510th Tank Battalion. But memories of frontier days were strong, and the 510th was redesignated the Tenth Cavalry in 1958 and stationed at Fort Knox, Kentucky.

A bronze statue in memory of the Ninth and Tenth Cavalry and the Twenty-fourth and Twenty-fifth Infantry was dedicated in 1992 at Fort Leavenworth, Kansas, to commemorate the courage of the Buffalo Soldiers and mark their place in American military history.

* * *

The Ninth and Tenth Cavalry served in Texas, New Mexico, Oklahoma, Nebraska, Utah, and Montana. In the 1880s their orders were to escort stagecoaches and survey parties through Indian territory. Black scouts like Isaiah Dorman, who fought at the Battle of the Little Bighorn, Frank Grouard, who led troops through Sioux country, and Sam Bowman, who could follow a trail through Apache territory, at different times accompanied the Buffalo soldiers. These men gave every ounce of their energy and skill to carry the mail, protect the railroads, clear off outlaws, and make the country safe for settlers. Hardest of all, Buffalo Soldiers were black men with orders to keep the peace between white men and red men. It was a daunting task.

The Ninth Cavalry was stationed at Fort Stockton in western Texas. Their quarters were austere—soldiers usually rested on sacks filled with straw and tossed across metal slats on a bunkbed. Their rations were poor and their horses seldom in top form. But the worst of it was that Stockton sat in the middle of the Great Comanche War Trail, a road used by the Kiowa and the Comanche to the north and the Apache to the south. The tribes warred with each other, with the Texans, and with a

Ninth Calvary in review, Fort Robinson, Nebraska, 1889

Company F, 25th Infantry, Fort Missoula, Montana

branch of the Kickapoo tribe living in Mexico. Against all odds, the Tenth helped capture the outlaw Billy the Kid and the dangerous Apache chief Geronimo. People said the men of the Tenth were part buffalo and part scorpion.

John J. Pershing, who would later lead U.S. Army forces in World War I, was a lieutenant when he took command of the Tenth Cavalry and earned the nickname Black Jack Pershing. He respected his troops and led them against the outlaw Pancho Villa in Mexico. During the Spanish-American War, Theodore Roosevelt, then an undersecretary of the navy, recruited a regiment of cowboys he called his Rough Riders. When the Rough Riders reached the top of San Juan Hill in Cuba, they found to their surprise that the Buffalo Soldiers were already there.[20]

Like their fellow soldiers in the cavalry, the Buffalo Soldiers in the Twenty-fourth and Twenty-fifth Infantry faced danger in the raw territories of Montana and Wyoming. Their job

Henry Flipper, first black graduate of West Point

was to protect the mail, guard stagecoach travelers, and fight outlaws and Indians. On one occasion, the Twenty-fourth was guarding an Army payroll in Arizona when it was ambushed by bandits. The paymaster recounted the fighting: "I was a soldier in Grant's old regiment, and during the entire [Civil] War it was justly proud of its record . . . but I never witnessed better courage or better fighting than shown by these colored soldiers on May 11, 1889. . . ."[21]

Because of their valor displayed in this fight, the United States government awarded Sergeant Benjamin Brown and Corporal Isaiah Mays, both of the Twenty-fourth Infantry, the Congressional Medal of Honor.

The Buffalo Soldiers helped to bring law and order to regions where ranchers fought with farmers, where Indian tribes warred with each other and with settlers, and where bandits threatened to overrun small towns. On rare occasions, settlers acknowledged their great debt to the black troops. When the Twenty-fifth was ordered to duty in the Spanish-American

War, the people of Missoula, Montana, postponed Easter church services so that they could line up along the town's main street and wave goodbye to the black troops who had become their protectors and friends.[22]

Over the years, that strange name, Buffalo Soldiers, became a prized possession of those black troops who left a legacy of courageous service in U.S. military history.

Serving under harsh conditions, these Buffalo Soldiers of the Tenth Calvary camped on Diamond Creek in New Mexico.

Mary Fields, "Stagecoach Mary"

Mary Fields was born in the 1830s in a slave cabin in Tennessee when Andrew Jackson was president. She was a strapping young woman, six feet tall, who could shoot a rifle and a six-shooter and handle a team of horses.

After her family died and the Civil War ended, Mary went to Toledo, Ohio. Then in 1884, when she was a woman of fifty, she went to Montana, where a friend who was an Ursuline nun lived in St. Peter's Mission, eight miles outside the town of Cascade. The nuns convinced the bishop to let Mary haul supplies from Cascade out to the mission. Mary was glad to have the job.

According to one story, when Mary was driving at night, a pack of hungry wolves came so close, they frightened her horses. The wagon spilled over on its side and the horses ran off. Mary was a cool-headed woman. She built a fire from sagebrush and kept the wolves off, first with her rifle and then with her revolver. At dawn, Mary set the wagon on its wheels and reloaded the supplies. Then she pulled the wagon into town herself.

Mary hauled freight for eight years. She was famous through the territory for the cigars she smoked and the jug of whiskey she kept on the wagon seat beside her.

Although Mary was a favorite of the town,

she lost her job hauling supplies for the nuns. It happened this way: She thought a hired hand had insulted her, and she challenged him to a shootout. He drew first but his shot went wild. Mary took slow and careful aim and fired just close enough to send him running. When the bishop heard about the contest, he was so angry he fired Mary. It was bad enough for men to go about shooting each other, but he couldn't accept women as gunslingers, too.

Mary got a new job driving the town's stagecoach, and that is how she came to be known as "Stagecoach Mary." She enjoyed working in the open air, and she was as good as any man at protecting her passengers and her cargo. After a time, Mary opened a restaurant, but she gave free meals to so many hungry travelers that her restaurant went broke. Customers thought it was just as well because they suspected she mixed gunshot in her stew.

Mary Fields was one of the first black women to carry the U.S. mail.

When the restaurant closed, Mary Fields was already in her sixties, but she decided she had better go back to work, and in 1895 she became the second woman in history to carry the United States mail.

At age seventy, Mary began to think she was too old for riding, and she opened a laundry. When a customer did not pay his laundry bill, Mary stopped him on the street and knocked him flat with her fist. Then she told him his bill was "settled."

She was a local celebrity by that time, and the mayor of Cascade gave her permission to drink in the all-male saloons. One of her old drinking partners remembered, "She could drink more whiskey than anyone I ever knew."

Mary was never a peaceful woman, but people had become so fond of her that public schools in Cascade closed on her birthday.

Mary died in 1914 and was buried at the Hillside Cemetery in Cascade, Montana, where a wooden cross marks her grave. But stories about Mary Fields never seem to die. There is always someone who remembers Mary, a fearless black woman who loved riding, shooting, and life on the western frontier.[23]

Mary Ellen Pleasant

Like many of the men and women whose stories are in this book, Mary Ellen Pleasant was born in the 1830s on a slave plantation in Georgia. She moved to Boston, married a free black man and together they crossed the country to California. In those days, San Francisco was as much a frontier town as Abilene or Dodge City, Kansas, but instead of cowboys, it was full of miners and railroad men.

Just before the start of the Civil War, the abolitionist John Brown was hiding somewhere in Canada, planning to lead an insurrection of slaves at Harper's Ferry in Virginia. It is said that the black community in San Francisco raised $30,000 to support his cause, and that the money was carried to his secret headquarters in 1858 by a black woman known as "Mammy" Pleasant.

At Harper's Ferry, John Brown armed a group of slaves, and there was heavy fighting. Brown was captured by the Virginia militia and a company of marines led by Colonel Robert E. Lee. He was tried, found guilty of treason, and hanged on December 12, 1859. Many considered Brown a madman, but the governor of Virginia said, "He is a man of clear head, of courage, of fortitude, and simple ingenuousness."[24] John Brown's act certainly hastened the start of the Civil War.

Home of Mary Ellen Pleasant

Although California was a free state, the rights of black citizens were far from secure. In San Francisco, with the war still going on, Mary Ellen Pleasant and two other black women did a daring thing. They filed a civil suit in San Francisco against a street-car company that had refused to let them ride because of their color. Surprisingly, the court supported their right to ride on public transportation in that city.[25] A century later, in 1955, another black woman, Rosa Parks, refused to move to the rear of a bus in Montgomery, Alabama. That simple act, some people believe, marked the beginning of the Civil Rights movement in America.

Mary Ellen Pleasant lived in San Francisco throughout her long life. She ran a boarding house, owned real estate, and was one of the founders of the black community in that city.

Biddy Mason was born a slave in 1818 in Hancock County, Georgia. She had three daughters, Harriet, Ann, and Ellen. As slaves in 1850, they were taken to California. They traveled by wagon at the end of a long caravan of three hundred wagons, where the dust from the hooves of the horses and the oxen was stifling. Biddy kept going because she knew that California was a free state where slavery was not recognized.

In 1856 the family who owned them decided to move from California with their slaves to Texas. But Biddy refused to go. She said she had become a free woman because she was living in a free state. Then she convinced the sheriff to stop her master from taking her out of California. With the help of white friends, she petitioned the federal district court in Los Angeles County, and in 1856 she was declared a free woman.

Biddy Mason was lucky. Other black men and women during the years preceding the Civil War were still considered "property" by most courts even when they had been taken to free territory. The legal issues were complicated because some states allowed slavery, others outlawed slavery, and territories had laws that were unclear. Dred Scott was a slave in

Missouri. His master took him to the free state of Illinois, then into territory where slavery had been excluded by the Missouri Compromise, and then back again to Missouri. Scott sued for his freedom because, like Biddy Mason, he said he had become a free man by living in Illinois. The Supreme Court, only one year after a court in Los Angeles found Biddy Mason was free, declared that Dred Scott had no right to bring suit because he was a slave and not a citizen. The court declared that the Missouri Compromise was unconstitutional because masters could take their slaves anywhere they liked. The Dred Scott decision, like John Brown's raid at Harper's Ferry, split the nation apart. "Thousands of people who had been indifferent were now persuaded that slavery must be abolished."[26] The black leader Frederick Douglass told his people that it was only a matter of time before "the complete overthrow of the whole slave system" would occur.[27]

Biddy Mason, pioneer and free black woman

Biddy Mason married Charles P. Owens in Los Angeles, and they worked together on behalf of the struggling black community. Biddy shrewdly guessed that in the long run land, not gold, was the most valuable thing to own, and she began buying real estate with every bit of money she could earn. She and her husband started with twelve lots, but by the end of the 1880s, Biddy Mason's estate was worth more than $200,000.

She used her money to help black families around her. She paid grocery bills when people were in need; she donated land for black schools, churches, and nursing homes; she sent food to black men in local jails; and she helped families devastated by floods. Biddy Mason did not leave a monument, but she left a black community in Los Angeles that has survived to the present day. When she died in 1891, one of those who knew her life's work called Biddy Mason one of the most remarkable pioneers of California.

Black Indians

Nineteenth century American society was built on legal codes that separated the black and white races. Runaway slaves throughout the South found refuge among what were called the "Five Civilized Tribes"—the Cherokee, Creek, Seminole, Chickasaw, and Choctaw. In those tribes, they married and raised families. They were called "mixed bloods," and most of them had the full rights of tribal members.

The history of "black Indians" is as varied as the tribes with which they lived. Sometimes blacks lived with the tribes and kept their identities intact. At other times, they simply considered themselves Indians. Sometimes runaway slaves joined Indian tribes as a way of fighting against the system that enslaved them. In 1861 an army of Creek braves fought side by side with three hundred blacks against the Confederacy. On the other hand, blacks who joined the Seminole Indians moved to Mexico and did not return until 1870, after the Civil War had ended. When they came back to Texas, they identified themselves as the Black Seminole Nation. The U.S. Army, patrolling a vast area of the Southwest against the Comanches, Kiowas, and Apaches, asked the Black Seminole to serve as guides. They formed a unit called the Seminole Negro Indian Scouts. They were desert fighters and

trackers, "probably the finest soldiers the U.S. Army ever sent into the field."[28] Chiefs John Horse and Snake Warrior led the scouts, three of whom were awarded the Congressional Medal of Honor.[29]

In 1882 Chief John Horse asked the U.S. government for land promised to the tribe in treaties. On behalf of his people he asked for "a home." There is no record of that request being honored. The Seminole Negro Indian Scouts were dissolved in 1914, and in 1970 a Seminole Negro Indian graveyard, the only land they received, was set aside outside of Bracketsville, Texas, as a final resting place for the men.[30]

Black Indians were men and women with divided loyalties. When one hundred thousand settlers overran Indian lands in Oklahoma in 1889, about ten thousand of those settlers, called "boomers," were African Americans who hoped to see Oklahoma become a black state. But black Indians, living in what had been called Indian territory, watched in

Diana Fletcher lived with the Kiowa people.

*Jim Taylor (left)
and a member of the
Ute tribe*

dismay as their lands were gobbled up. When Oklahoma came into the Union in 1907 as the forty-sixth state, it was clear that neither black Indians nor black Americans would find a safe haven—segregation was ordered in schools, railroad cars, and public buildings. "Oklahoma became the first state to segregate telephone booths."[31]

The Chippewa, Sioux, Ute, Kiowa, Comanche, and Sauk and Fox all had black tribal members. Scattered photographs of men and women testify that blacks and Indians lived together as families and as tribes. African Americans today often trace their family roots not only back to Africa but to the tribes of the American Indians as well.

Kitty Cloud Taylor (standing), wife of John Taylor, and her Ute sister. Both women are shown with their children.

*Little girl in
Tonepah, Nevada,
about 1900*

Conclusion

It would be wrong to suggest that the frontier was without prejudice. It had its share of violence and racial injustice. As settlements grew into cities, Jim Crow segregation laws confronted black settlers. But on those lonely, dangerous, and beautiful lands we call the frontier, black pioneers built new lives. Born into slavery, African Americans had the same dreams of freedom and independence as did all other Americans. Given the chance, they proved time and again that they possessed skills, initiative, and courage.

West of the Mississippi, between 1850 and 1900, there were some ten thousand African American exodusters, homesteaders, and sod busters. There were also four thousand miners, eight thousand wranglers and rodeo riders, and some five thousand Buffalo Soldiers. According to some historians, there were some eighty thousand African Americans doing whatever else the frontier demanded. They were trappers and mountain men, hotel keepers, and scouts. They were businessmen and women, teachers, and nurses.

And they were cowboys. From the Chisholm Trail to Hollywood, the American cowboy is a hero who walks tall. It is important to remember, then, that some of America's best cowboys and rodeo riders were black, and that some of our bravest pioneers were African Americans who lived and worked on America's western frontiers.

Notes

1. NELL IRVIN PAINTER, *Exodusters: Black Migration to Kansas After Reconstruction* (New York: Alfred A. Knopf, 1976), 4.
2. IBID., 114.
3. U.S. DEPARTMENT OF THE INTERIOR/NATIONAL PARK SERVICE, *Promised Land on the Solomon: Black Settlement at Nicodemus, Kansas* (Washington, D.C., n.d.), 1.
4. FRANK DOBIE, *The Longhorns* (Austin, Tex.: University of Texas Press, 1980), 92.
5. JACK WESTON, *The Real American Cowboy* (New York: Schocken Books, 1985), 165.
6. NAT LOVE, *The Life and Adventures of Nat Love* (Los Angeles, 1907; reprint, Baltimore: Black Classic Press, 1988), 47–49; all citations from this edition.
7. IBID., 97.
8. IBID., 99.
9. IBID., 99–100.
10. IBID., 104.
11. IBID., 114.
12. IBID., 115.
13. IBID., 107.
14. IBID., 161–162.
15. COLONEL BAILEY C. HANES, *Bill Pickett, Bulldogger* (Norman, Okla: University of Oklahoma Press, 1977), 44.
16. IBID., 58–60.
17. IBID., 186.
18. PHILIP DURHAM AND EVERETT L. JONES, *The Negro Cowboys* (New York: Dodd Mead, 1965), 181.

19. WILLIAM LOREN KATZ, *The Black West*, 3d ed. (Seattle, Wash.: Open Hand Publishing Inc., 1987), 161. William Loren Katz deserves special note for his work in this field.

20. IBID., 272–273.

21. IBID., 217.

22. IBID., 219.

23. MARC CRAWFORD, "Stagecoach Mary," as told by Gary Cooper. *Ebony Magazine* (October 1977; reprint from original publication, October 1959), 96–98, 100, 102.

24. JOHN HOPE FRANKLIN, *From Slavery to Freedom*, 4th ed. (New York: Alfred A. Knopf, 1973), 211.

25. LAWRENCE B. DE GRAAF, "Race, Sex, and Region: Black Women in the American West, 1850–1920," *Pacific Historical Review* 49 (May 1980): 292. W. Sherman Savage, *Blacks in the West* (Westport, Conn.: Greenwood Press, 1976), 152–153.

26. FRANKLIN, op. cit., 210.

27. IBID., 212.

28. WILLIAM LOREN KATZ, *Black Indians: A Hidden Heritage* (New York: Atheneum Press, 1986), 79.

29. IBID., 82.

30. IBID., 87–88.

31. IBID., 152.

Bibliography

BEASLEY, DELILAH L. *The Negro Trail Blazers of California*. 1919, reprinted New York: Negro Universities Press, 1969.

BONNER, T.D., ed., *The Life and Adventures of James P. Beckwourth*. 1856, reprinted New York: Arno Press, 1969.

DE GRAAF, LAWRENCE B. "Race, Sex, and Region: Black Women in the American West, 1850–1920," *Pacific Historical Review* 49 (May 1980), 285–313.

DOBIE, FRANK. *The Longhorns*. Austin, Tex.: University of Texas Press, 1980.

DURHAM, PHILIP, and EVERETT L. JONES. *The Negro Cowboys*. New York: Dodd Mead, 1965.

FRANKLIN, JOHN HOPE. *From Slavery to Freedom*. 4th ed. New York: Alfred A. Knopf, 1973.

HANES, COLONEL BAILEY C. *Bill Pickett, Bulldogger*. Norman, Okla.: University of Oklahoma Press, 1977.

KATZ, WILLIAM LOREN. *Black Indians: A Hidden Heritage*. New York: Atheneum Press, 1986.

——*The Black West*. 3d ed. Seattle, Wash.: Open Hand Publishing Inc., 1987.

KNAPP, MAJOR GEORGE E. *Buffalo Soldiers at Fort Leavenworth in the 1930s and early 1940s*. Combat Studies Institute, U.S. Army Command College, Fort Leavenworth, Kansas, 1991.

LAPP, RUDOLPH M. *Blacks in the Gold Rush in California.* New Haven, Conn.: Yale University Press, 1977.

LECKIE, WILLIAM H. *The Buffalo Soldiers.* Norman, Okla.: University of Oklahoma Press, 1967.

LOVE, NAT. *The Life and Adventures of Nat Love.* 1907, reprinted; Baltimore: Black Classic Press, 1988.

PAINTER, NELL Irvin. *Exodusters: Black Migration to Kansas After Reconstruction.* New York: Alfred A. Knopf, 1976.

PORTER, KENNETH W. *The Negro on the American Frontier.* New York: Arno Press, 1970.

RILEY, GLENDA. "American Daughters: Black Women in the West," *Montana Magazine of Western History* 38 (Spring 1988), 14–27.

SAVAGE, W. SHERMAN. *Blacks in the West.* Westport, Conn.: Greenwood Press, 1976.

U.S. DEPARTMENT OF THE INTERIOR/NATIONAL PARK SERVICE. *Promised Land on the Solomon: Black Settlement at Nicodemus, Kansas.* Washington, D.C., n.d.

MUSEUMS OF BLACK WESTERN HISTORY:

Black American West Museum
and Heritage Center
3091 California Street
Denver, Colo. 80205

Great Plains Black Museum
2213 Lake Street
Omaha, Neb. 68110

Picture Credits

Baltimore: Black Classic Press: 35

Black American West Museum, Paul W. Stewart Collection: 40 (left), 61

Buffalo Bill Historical Center, Cody, WY: 30

Solomon D. Butcher Collection, Nebraska State Historical Society: 18, 24, 25

California Section, California State Library: 51, 52, 64

Center for Southwest Research, General Library, University of New Mexico: 59

Collections of the Library of Congress: back jacket, 15

Colorado Historical Society: 6

Arthur Cromwell, courtesy of Nebraska State Historical Society: 130

Denver Public Library, Western History Department: 12, 42, 49, 53, 70

Thomas Gilcrease Museum, Tulsa, OK: 29

Kansas State Historical Society: 17,19,22,23

National Archives: 55, 58

National Baseball Library, Cooperstown, NY: 27

Nebraska State Historical Society: frontispiece, 8, 20, 32, 40 (right), 56, 57, 71

Nevada Historical Society: 26, 39, 72

Seaver Center for Western History Research, Natural History Museum of Los Angeles County: 66

Western History Collections, University of Oklahoma Library: 37, 69

Index

Abilene, Kansas, 28, 63
Africa, 71
Alabama, 30
Allen, Virge, 18
Apache Indians, 54, 56, 68
Arizona, 36, 58
Arkansas, 41
Astor, John Jacob, 9
Auburn Ravine, California, 52
Austin, Texas, 36

Beadle, Erastus, 44
Beckwourth, Jim, 11–13
Billy the Kid. See Bonney,
    William
Black Seminole Indians, 68–69
Blackfoot Indians, 11, 12
Boley, Oklahoma, 23
Bonga family, 9-10
Bonney, William, 34, 57
Boston, Massachusetts, 63
Bowman, Sam, 55
Bracketsville, Texas, 69
Bronco Jim, 31
Brown, Benjamin, 58

Brown, Clara, 51
Brown, John, 63, 66
Brown, Maurice, 20
Brownlee, Nebraska, 2
Bruce, Joe, 44-49
Buffalo Bill, 44
Bush, George Washington, 23

Calamity Jane, 44
California, 50, 63, 64, 65, 67
California Territory, 12
Canada, 38, 63
Cascade, Montana, 60, 62
Central America, 50
Central Park Zoo (New York
    City), 34
Cherokee Indians, 68
Cherry County, Nebraska, 2
Cheyenne, Wyoming, 36, 52
Cheyenne Indians, 11, 54
Chicago, 28, 50
Chicago, Illinois, 28, 50
Chickasaw Indians, 68
Chippewa Indians, 71
Chisholm Trail, 73

Choctaw Indians, 68
Clark, William, 9
Colorado, 12, 30, 50, 51, 52
Comanche Indians, 54, 56, 68, 71
Creek Indians, 68
Crow Indians, 11, 12, 13
Custer, George Armstrong, 32, 54
Custer County, Nebraska, 18, 24,
    25

Dart, Isom or Isham. See
    Huddleston, Ned
Deadwood, South Dakota, 32
Deadwood Dick. See Love, Nat
Denver, Colorado, 39, 40, 52, 53
Diamond Creek (New Mexico),
    59
Dismal River (Kansas), 17
Dodge City, Kansas, 28, 31, 34, 63
Dorman, Isaiah, 55
Douglass, Frederick, 50, 66
Dunlap, Kansas, 21, 22, 23, 25

Ebony Star, 45-49
England, 9. See also Great Britain

Fields, Mary, 60-62
Fletcher, Diana, 69
Flipper, Henry, 58
Florida, 11
Ford, Barney, 50-52
Fort Dodge, Kansas, 34
Fort Knox, Kentucky, 55
Fort Leavenworth, Kansas, 55
Fort Missoula, Nebraska, 57
Fort Robinson, Nebraska, 56
Fort Stockton, Texas, 56
France, 9
Frémont, John Charles, 12

Georgia, 63
Geronimo, 38, 57
Grant, Ulysses S., 54, 58
Great Britain, 38. See also
    England
Great Comanche War Trail,
    56
Great Lakes, 9
Great Plains, 7
Grierson, Benjamin, 54
Grouard, Frank, 55

Hancock County, Georgia, 65
Harper's Ferry, Virginia, 63, 66
Hatch, Edward, 54
Horn, Tom, 43
Horse, John, 69
Houston, Texas, 39
Huddleston, Ned, 41–43, 49
Hudson River, 9
Hurricane Nell, 44

Illinois, 66
Ingraham, Prentiss, 44

Jackson, Andrew, 60
Jefferson, Thomas, 9
John Horse. *See* Horse, John

Kansas, 15, 16, 21, 22, 34
Kickapoo Indians, 57
Kiowa Indians, 54, 56, 68, 69, 71

Lakin, Kansas, 19
Langston, Oklahoma, 23
Lee, Robert E., 63
Lewis, Meriwether, 9
Lone Ranger, 49
Los Angeles, California, 66, 67
Los Angeles County, California, 65
Louisiana, 14, 25
Love, Nat, 31–35, 44

McColl, Ada, 19
McCrea, Joel, 39
Mason, Biddy, 65–67
Masterson, Bat, 34
Mays, Isaiah, 58

Mexico, 12, 41, 57, 68
Minnesota Territory, 10
Mississippi River, 9, 14, 15, 73
Missoula, Montana, 59
Missouri, 66
Missouri River, 9
Mix, Tom, 38
Montana, 32, 55, 57, 60
Montgomery, Alabama, 64
Mountain City, Colorado, 51
Mulhall, Lucille, 38

National Rodeo Cowboy Hall of Fame, 39
Nebraska, 16, 23, 55
Netherlands, 9
Nevada, 25
New Mexico, 55
New York, New York, 34, 40, 44, 50
Nicaragua, 50
Nicodemus, Kansas, 21, 23, 25
North America, 9
North Dakota, 16

Oklahoma, 23, 38, 42, 55, 69, 70
Oklahoma City, Oklahoma, 38, 39
Oklahoma Territory, 37
Omohundro, Texas Jack, 45-49
101 Ranch, 37-38
Oregon Territory, 23
Owens, Charles P., 67

Pacific Ocean, 9
Paige, Satchell, 25, 27
Panama Canal, 50
Parks, Rosa, 64

Pershing, Black Jack. *See* Pershing, John J.
Pershing, John J., 57
Pickett, Bill, 36-39, 40, 49
Pickett, Thomas Jefferson, 36
Pleasant, Mary Ellen, 63-64
Puget Sound, 23

Remington, Frederic, 29
Reno, Nevada, 13
Rocky Mountains, 11, 12
Roosevelt, Theodore, 57
Rose, Edward, 9

Sacajawea, 9
St. Lawrence River, 9
San Francisco, California, 50, 63, 64
San Juan Hill (Cuba), 57
Santa Fe Trail, 12
Sauk and Fox Indians, 71
Scott, Dred, 65-66
Seminole Indians, 11, 68. *See also* Black Seminole Indians
Sheridan, Philip, 54
Sherman, William Tecumseh, 54
Shores family, 24, 25
South Loup River (Nebraska), 18
Sierra Nevada, 12
Singleton, Benjamin, 21, 22
Sioux Indians, 32, 54, 71
Snake Indians, 12
Snake Warrior, 69
Solomon, John Lewis, 14-15
South America, 38
South Carolina, 30
South Dakota, 16

Spanish Flat, California, 51
Speese, Moses, 25
Stahl, Jesse, 39, 40
Sutter's Mill (California), 12

Taft, Oklahoma, 23
Taylor, Jim, 70
Taylor, John, 71
Taylor, Kitty Cloud, 71
Tennessee, 21, 31, 60
Texas, 25, 28, 30, 31, 33, 34, 36, 44, 55, 65, 68
Texas Jack. *See* Omohundro, Texas Jack
Thomas County, Kansas, 17
Toledo, Ohio, 60
Tonepah, Nevada, 26, 72
Tonto, 49
Tulsa, Oklahoma, 38

United States, 38, 41
Utah, 55
Ute Indians, 54, 70, 71

Villa, Pancho, 57
Virginia, 11, 63

Wagoner, Henry, 50, 52
Wagoner, Julia, 50
Walker, Arthur L., 40
Westville, Nebraska, 24, 25
Wichita, Kansas, 28, 38
Wisconsin Territory, 10
Wyoming, 57

York (slave on Lewis and Clark expedition), 9